ADVENTURES
OF THE
BASS BUDDIES

TALES OF FUN, FOLLY, FRIENDSHIP,
FAITH, AND A LITTLE FISHING

JUSTIN BURGSTINER
ROBERT TAYLOR
EARL BAGLEY
BERNIE BROWN

InspiringVoices®

Copyright © 2015 Bernie Brown.

All rights reserved. No part of this book may be used or reproduced by any means, graphic, electronic, or mechanical, including photocopying, recording, taping or by any information storage retrieval system without the written permission of the publisher except in the case of brief quotations embodied in critical articles and reviews.

Inspiring Voices books may be ordered through booksellers or by contacting:

Inspiring Voices
1663 Liberty Drive
Bloomington, IN 47403
www.inspiringvoices.com
1 (866) 697-5313

Because of the dynamic nature of the Internet, any web addresses or links contained in this book may have changed since publication and may no longer be valid. The views expressed in this work are solely those of the author and do not necessarily reflect the views of the publisher, and the publisher hereby disclaims any responsibility for them.

Any people depicted in stock imagery provided by Thinkstock are models, and such images are being used for illustrative purposes only. Certain stock imagery © Thinkstock.

ISBN: 978-1-4624-1147-4 (sc)
ISBN: 978-1-4624-1148-1 (e)

Library of Congress Control Number: 2015911795

Print information available on the last page.

Inspiring Voices rev. date: 08/11/2015

Contents

Foreword xi
In Memoriam xv
Acknowledgments xvii
Introduction xix
In the Beginning xxi

Chapter 1: The Country 1
    The Cabin 2
    The Pond 3
    The River 4
    The Cowarts' 5

Chapter 2: The Early Adventures 7
    A Naked Catch 8
    Catch the Bus 9
    Well-Done Burger 11
    What's That Smell? 12
    Guests in Our Bedroom 13
    Cut Off His Shirttail 15

Chapter 3: Who Are the Bass Buddies? 19

Chapter 4: Earl 21
    Tawny Port 21
    Backing the Trailer 22
    Is He Alive? 24
    No Water 25
    My Best Catch 26
    What It Meant to Me 27

Chapter 5: Justin 29
    Sinking the Boat: Our Conversion 29
    The Different Boats 31
    Stuck Like a Bullfrog 32
    The Fly Sting 33
    My New Friend 34
    My Best Catch 35
    What It Meant to Me 35

Chapter 6: Bernie 37
    An Explosive Dinner 37
    Sons-in-Law 39
    It's Going To Be All Right 40
    The Pécan 41
    How Much Grits? 43
    Best Catch 44
    What It Meant to Me 46

Chapter 7: Robert 49
    The Car Is Locked 49
    A Light Supper 51
    The Ugly Lure 52
    Trolling for Bream 53

  Best Catch 55
  What It Meant to Me 56

Chapter 8: The Alternates 59
  John Bowling... 60
  Bucky Smith 61
  Richard Hubbard 63
  Whit Byram 64
  Ryon Rambo 65
  Brad Mclean 67

Reflections and Conclusions 71
Bass Buddies' Photo Album.. 75
Bass Buddies' Mounted Trophies.. 79
Bass Buddies' Art Gallery 83
Books By Bernie Brown 85

ADVENTURES

OF THE

BASS BUDDIES

Tales of Fun, Folly, Friendship,
Faith, and a Little Fishing

*May your own adventures bring much joy and
provide you with tales to share!*

Justin Burgstiner

Robert Taylor

Earl Bagley

Bernie Brown

Foreword

FISHING IS MORE THAN catching fish. It's a distraction from the cares of the world; it's an activity where relationships with others can be formed and nurtured; it's an opportunity to observe the wonders of God's creation. And it's a time when experiences can grow into lasting stories and tales. Fishing is medicine for the body, mind, and soul.

Adventures of the Bass Buddies captures the essence of what fishing is all about. It is amazing that four individuals have maintained the practice of fishing together in one place so long—two for over sixty years. The tales that the "Bass Buddies" share with you will at times make you smile, laugh, reflect, and even shed a tear. Actually, they are probably better storytellers than fishermen.

Having spent my life as a fisherman, I believe that I'm qualified to recommend a good read on this subject. You won't be wasting your time to partake of what this little book has to offer. It may be the "medicine" that you need right now; it might even be your catch of the day!

Jimmy Houston
Professional Fisherman, Television Personality and Author

From the Lady Who Still Calls Us "My Boys"

WHEN MY HUSBAND, E.L., and I moved from the city of Savannah out to join our friend Aunt Louise in what we called "the country," we experienced many new adventures of our own. Some of the most enjoyable and fulfilling aspects of this rural lifestyle were visits from family and friends seeking renewal and respite from the stresses, strains, and demands of modern life. In one particular case, I was able to observe two young boys grow and mature all the way from childhood to senior citizens. Along the way, they had two others join them to form a special and unique bond that has now lasted over sixty years. In a way, I look at them as "my boys" because they spent many of their favorite times with us. Justin, Bernie, Robert, and Earl have some interesting and fascinating stories to tell. We often sat on the porch of the cabin and not only shared the happenings of the day but also solved many of the ills of the world. Looking back, if some of the world leaders had joined us, we probably wouldn't have as many societal problems as we have today.

We learned a lot from this small group of buddies, and we taught them a thing or two. Let me give you one example. In an isolated setting such as this, we didn't waste anything. The boys would always fillet the bass that they caught. So I would ask them to save the center bones that still had some meat on them. After boiling these, the meat just fell off and was used for fish gumbo as an appetizer for our meals. In time, something that was once discarded became a regularly requested item on the menu. There's probably a sermon here.

I think that one of the main attractions of country living is the simplicity that accompanies it. Time just seems to slow down. We tend to be distracted from many of those things that worry us most, and even our conversations are uplifting. Smiles become more prevalent than frowns, and God seems a little closer.

I've listened to the Bass Buddies' tales for over sixty years, and I'm glad that they have finally written some of them down so you can enjoy them too.

Teeny Cowart*

*Teeny lived many years in "the country" where these adventures took place. At ninety-five, she represents the generation that helped raise the Bass Buddies.

In Memoriam

Carolyn Burgstiner

1940–2014

Bass Buddies' Wives

Carolyn Burgstiner, Snookie Brown, Suzanne Taylor, and Betsy Bagley.

Acknowledgments

FIRST, WE OWE A debt of gratitude to Uncle John, Aunt Louise, E.L., and Teeny for always treating us like family when we visited the country. And special thanks to Teeny, who is still with us, for her message of support and encouragement above.

Second, we sincerely appreciate our new Bass Buddy, Jimmy Houston, for his foreword. This is particularly special to us because we used his wonderful book, *Hooked for Life,* for devotionals on several of our trips.

Third, we thank our publisher, *Inspiring Voices,* for the assistance of a great team that helped us record our experiences (tales) not just for others but also for ourselves.

And finally, to our wives who not only allowed but also encouraged us to take these special fishing trips each year—our thanks and love.

—The Bass Buddies

Introduction

WE ARE RECORDING OUR adventures in this little book with heavy hearts. Due to the many issues that accompany the aging process, we may be closing a very important chapter in our lives. But this will not keep us from continuing to share our experiences, our tales. It all started like a Mark Twain novel, but the Tom Sawyers and Huckleberry Finns in our stories have never grown up. Though we all have now passed the seventy-year marker, we are still just boys at heart. Our enthusiasm and passion for adventure have not waned one iota.

We call ourselves the "Bass Buddies" because our prey is the largemouth bass that inhabit the dark waters of the ponds, lakes, and rivers of south Georgia. We claim to be fishermen, but a more accurate title might be storytellers. The stories you are about to read have been shared often over the years, but this is the first time most have been recorded on printed pages. Some have asked if they are absolutely and literally true. To our knowledge, they are, though distortions and exaggerations can creep in. However, we fall back on an old adage: truth is often stranger than fiction.

We thank those of you who join us in these recollections. We remind you that there are four of us. Each has his own style and way of expressing himself. Though we have some things in common, we differ in personalities and experiences. This is an account of our relationship together over many years and the appreciation and respect that we have for each other. We view this little volume as more than a fishing storybook; it is our testimony to one of God's greatest gifts: the capacity for brotherly love. And fishermen may be inherently gifted in this regard. Remember Jesus called several fishermen to be his disciple buddies, and they shared many stories with us.

In the Beginning

EVERY TALE HAS A beginning. This one started in the early 1950s. Two families had just moved to Savannah, Georgia, and were settling in. Frank Burgstiner was transferred to Savannah by the telephone company. He, Jessie, and their two boys were glad to be back home with family and many old friends. Justin was the oldest son. During the same year, Reverend Bernard Brown was appointed minister at the Trinity Methodist Church in the downtown area. Bernard, Elizabeth, and their three children (at the time) moved into the parsonage just a few blocks from the church. Bernie was the oldest and only son.

From these two events, an unlikely friendship began between Justin and Bernie. Bernie was a couple of years older, and the two boys lived in different neighborhoods and went to different schools. But they had one thing in common: they both attended the same church, and their parents were adamant about the children participating in all the activities there. Therefore, they were thrown together at worship services, Sunday school, youth fellowship, choir, boy scouts, camps, etc.

Justin's mother had a sister named Louise who was married to John Deason. John owned a service (we called it a filling) station where the two boys had their first jobs—pumping gas and washing car windshields. Both John and Louise were pillars in the Trinity church. The Deasons also had some family property in the adjacent country that bordered on the Savannah River. They called this land "the country." A few years earlier, John had dammed up a stream that led down to the river and created a lake that they called "the pond." John and Louise had no children of their own but had hundreds of nieces and nephews; everyone called them "Uncle" John and "Aunt" Louise. Justin was already a true nephew, and Bernie was quickly adopted into the family. All this led to regular visits by the two boys to the "country" as they tagged along with just about everyone who was going there. Almost immediately, Bernie became an avid fisherman. But that bug didn't bite Justin as quickly.

Located on the property was an old hunters' and loggers' cabin that had been erected many years earlier. Timber was cut on the property and floated down the Savannah River to mills for lumber, paper, etc. John and Louise made this their country home and simply called it "the cabin."

Many years later, after John died, Louise deeded a lot on the property to her dear friends E.L. and Teeny Cowart, who built a small house adjacent to the cabin. We called it "the Cowarts' house," but later it would become "the cabin" after the original one was struck by lightning and burned down.

This is the setting where the following adventures took place. Today, over sixty years later, the two boys and their buddies who joined them still view this wonderful place as hallowed ground. It was here that stories were born, friendships were deepened, and memories were filed in their minds forever.

Aunt Louise snapping beans; Teeny at supper; E.L. in conversation.

Chapter 1

The Country

WHERE IS "THE COUNTRY?" Here are the driving directions. It's located between Kildare and Clyo. From I-95N, take the last exit in Georgia before crossing into South Carolina. Travel through Rincon and Springfield to Kildare; turn right at Tommy's Store onto the Kildare-Clyo Road. After passing Mizpah Church and crossing the branch about halfway to Clyo, turn left onto the dirt road across from the volunteer fire station. This will dead-end at the next crossroad. Proceed straight across through the gate and follow the tire-track road for about a mile to the cabin. If you think this seems complicated or remote, you should have been there sixty years ago. Some of these roads didn't exist, and most were not paved.

When entering the country, you pass by three fields under cultivation; then you see a large forest or wooded area. Beyond the cabin, you follow the winding bumpy road down to the pond. There is a constant flow through the spillway at the dam down to the river. Wild game, including quail, dove, turkey, squirrel, deer, duck, and even alligator, are often spotted. The terrain ranges from flat to hilly with several ravines meandering throughout the almost four hundred acres of natural landscaped property. It would be hard not to believe in God in a place like this. His presence is obvious everywhere. Who else could have painted such a beautiful canvas for us to enjoy?

The Cabin

The cabin was initially built for hunters but was also used by loggers who floated logs they harvested down the Savannah River. It sits up on a bluff overlooking the river. Originally, it had only a couple of rooms with a wood stove for both heating and cooking. Bunk beds hung from most every wall. Its primary purpose was to provide a place for the crews to eat and sleep.

Uncle John, who majored in creativity and innovation, updated it with such modern conveniences as electricity and running water. First, a bank of automobile batteries from his service station were charged by a gasoline generator, connected to a DC wiring system taken from a ship, and installed inside the cabin for lighting. Second, these also powered a pump that drew water up from a well to a raised tank. Gravity from that provided enough water pressure for a sink inside. And third, a gas tank was the source of heat for a stove and some outside lighting. Even with all this, the cabin still had no inside plumbing for toilet or bath. This meant the only bathroom was the great outdoors, which included bathing in the pond or at nearby ice-cold Blue Springs. Later, an electric line was run from the main road to bring the cabin into the twentieth century. With this came a bathroom with shower and some additional space, including two porches. This might sound too basic and a bit archaic, but to a couple of teenage boys in the 1950s, it was a place for unmatched fun and adventure.

The Pond

The topography of the land adjacent to the river is interesting. In contrast to the flat fields and wooded areas near the entrance to the property, this section is quite hilly with ravines throughout. A stream fed by springs ran through one of the deepest valleys; a dam would make this the perfect lakebed. So here is where the pond was born. Evidently, enough resources weren't available at the time to remove all the timber that stood there, so trees remained standing to die a slow death as the water rose and their roots drowned. Over the years, they all ultimately fell and many sank to the bottom, creating an ideal habitat for the fish and other water creatures who would call this home. The pond created by the damming of the creek is only sixteen acres but seems much larger. It is long and narrow with many tributaries feeding into the main channel. Initially, it was stocked with bass and bream that have flourished over time; restocking has not been needed over the ensuing sixty-plus years.

The adjacent woods on this site are filled with all the native hardwood and softwood trees, and the long shore is lined with overhanging floral glory. Even during times of drought, the constant trickle from the feeding springs can be seen and heard. It is hard to find words to describe the beauty and majesty of this tranquil place of stilled waters nestled beside the great river that separates two states.

The River

There is a continuous stream measuring about two hundred yards from the pond's spillway down to the river, which is officially called the Savannah River. This magnificent body of water flows from above Augusta, through Savannah, and into the Atlantic Ocean. As we look across, we view the equally beautiful South Carolina shoreline; in this area, the river is the separating boundary between Georgia and South Carolina. This particular point is called Porter's Landing, named for ancestors of Aunt Louise and Justin's mother, Jessie.

Another interesting feature of this juncture along the river is a narrow canal that was dug many years ago to catch and control the logs as they slid down the bank. It's called Timber Creek. This resulted in an island of almost a hundred acres being created along the river. In the early days, a bridge to it was usually a fallen tree trunk that spanned the creek. It was eerie to explore the island with all its undisturbed grandeur; few humans have set foot on it in the past fifty years.

The Savannah River is swift and wide and difficult to fish except in coves and inlets. However, lines baited with small bream could be strung from overhanging trees and bushes along the bank and checked regularly. Frank Burgstiner, Justin's dad, caught one of the largest bass recorded in the area using this technique. The largemouth weighted seventeen pounds and was featured on a local sports program in the 1950s when television was relatively new. In contrast to the still waters of the pond, the current of the river is always fast and furious. Lessons abound when you stop and listen to the teaching of the Creator of this special place. There is a time to be still and a time to keep moving.

The Cowarts'

After Uncle John's death, Aunt Louise decided to make the cabin at the country her part-time home. Two of her closest friends were E.L. and Teeny Cowart, who loved rural life just like she did; he was a retired bank executive. Like the Deasons, the Cowarts had been active members of Trinity Methodist Church for many years. A lot next to the cabin was deeded to them where they built a small, two-bedroom house and later added a guest room and bath on the back. It became known as "the Cowarts'." At first, they maintained their home in Savannah, but a short time later, they moved permanently to the country, as did Aunt Louise. Trips to the country meant visits with these very special folks, which was a joy in itself.

They all resided there for almost twenty years before moving to independent living facilities near Savannah. Soon after that, Aunt Louise's cabin was struck by lightning and burned to the ground. A family corporation was set up to manage the property. Her last visit to her former home to see the charred remains of her beloved cabin marked the beginning of declining health, and she died soon afterward. The corporation then acquired the Cowarts' home and made it a part of the country estate. Today, it is now called "the cabin."

Over the years, a visit to the country was more than a fishing trip. Even now, the spirits of Uncle John, Aunt Louise, E.L., and Teeny Cowart are present there. They all had perfected the gift of hospitality and always made visitors feel welcome and important. They not only shared their beautiful place but also themselves. There is no doubt that we all are better people having been to "the country."

(Top) Cabin; (Middle) Pond; (Bottom) River

Chapter 2

The Early Adventures

THE EARLY ADVENTURES LASTED about six years; these tales took place during the mid-1950s. Many seniors like us still look back on the fifties as being the good old days. You could dance to the music; kids played outside; neighbors knew each other; most movies would be rated G; most families went to church on Sunday; life was fun and much more innocent in comparison to today; and on and on. For teenage boys like us this was a great time to grow up and test our wings. Probably most grown folks tell stories from their youth, so we are no different. Ours may be somewhat unique because so many of our adventures revolved around visits to one particular place and our growing interest in one activity: fishing.

The ringleaders were the two of us: Justin and Bernie. We enlisted many of our friends from our neighborhoods, schools, and church as accomplices. During this time, we graduated from adolescence and moved through our high school years. We learned to drive, got our first jobs and cars, tried out a cigarette and a beer, grew more hair, and kissed our first girls. And despite many other adventurous pursuits that you won't find recorded here, we survived.

We do want to share a few tales of our adventures that occurred during this period. From these, you will better understand why sixty-plus years later we still revere these memories. We feel blessed to have experienced such a special place, with special people, during a special period of time. We view this not as a coincidence but as a God incidence, and we will be forever thankful.

A Naked Catch

It was a Friday night when I (Bernie) got a call from Justin's dad, Frank. (He was "Mr. Burgstiner" to me at the time.) He was asking if I would like to go up to the country with him the next morning. I did this from time to time because Justin was not much of a fisherman when we were young teenagers. Of course, I was always ready to go there with anyone at any time. Frank was the best fisherman that I had ever met. In those days, we fished with cane poles.

Our pattern was to fish for bream off the dam and, when we caught a small one, use it as live bait for bass. A long pole was stuck in the ground with a float and the baitfish on a large hook. We were down shore when we heard a loud splash; a bass had struck the bait and pulled the pole out of the ground. We could see only a few inches of it as it shot toward the middle of the pond. It was in an open area so there was nothing to hang up the line.

"Bernie, swim out there and get him!" Frank yelled.

"I don't have a bathing suit or extra clothes," I answered.

"Take your clothes off, and go get it. Looks like a big one" came his instructions.

I would never do this today, but I took everything off and dove into the water. It took a while to catch up with the pole, and the fish had no intention of coming peacefully back to the shore. But finally, I prevailed, and I handed the pole to Frank, who proceeded to drag it out of the water. He was right. It was a big one—the largest bass that I had ever seen at the time.

Then disaster struck; either the line broke or the flailing of the fish dislodged the hook. It came sliding down the steep bank back toward the water just as I was coming out—we met at the water's edge. At the movies, I had seen Tarzan wrestle a crocodile with just his shorts on. But that seemed tame compared to me taking on a large largemouth bass with nothing on. I don't know what drove me most: a desire for self-preservation or landing that monster fish. Somehow though, I was able to drag it back up on the shore. We had no camera back then and Frank died many years ago, so this tale is only documented by the fact that I brought an eight-pounder home that my mom baked and served our entire family.

Catch the Bus

In the early days (1950s), kids could do things that they just can't do today. Here's one example.

As on most weekends, Justin and Bernie hitched a ride up to the country on Friday afternoon and were planning to return on Saturday evening. The youth choir was singing at the Sunday morning service, and they were required to be there. For some reason, Uncle John didn't understand the boys had this command performance and had planned to stay over until Sunday with the other guests who were there. John was always resourceful, so once he understood the dilemma, he came up with a creative solution. "I'll take you boys over to Kildare to catch the bus back to Savannah," he told them.

So after supper and just before dark, they were transported to Kildare. Now envision this: downtown Kildare was only a one-business establishment: Tommy's Store where the Clyo-Kildare Road intersected with the highway to Savannah (GA-21). There was not even a traffic light. The little store was already closed when they arrived. They were left with a flashlight and told to signal the bus to pick them up. It was due to come by in the next hour or so but would not stop unless the driver saw the flashing signal. By now it was dark, and they could not distinguish between large semitrailer trucks and a bus coming around the curve. So more than two dozen of these trucks received the signals before the big Greyhound rounded the curve. You can't imagine how relieved they were to step up into that bus and pay the one-dollar fare.

In those days, there were no cellphones or even a line phone at the country. And none of their parents back home knew exactly where the boys were or when they planned to return. Consequently, no one came downtown to the bus station to pick them up. Fortunately, Bernie's home in the parsonage was less than a couple of miles away. So about eleven o'clock, they had to hike through some of the roughest sections of town. By the time they made it to the parsonage, it was almost midnight and everyone had already gone to bed. Bernie's dad had to preach the next day and always retired early on Saturday night. They used the hidden key to get in the house and quietly went directly to Bernie's room—and then straight to bed.

The next morning, the boys got up and went downstairs. Bernie's mom was probably one of the calmest and most collected persons you will ever meet. But she just about had a heart attack when the two boys walked in the kitchen and asked, "What's for breakfast?" At the time, they chose not to give all the details of the previous night but just said that they had caught a ride home and came in after everyone was asleep. They realized that to tell the whole truth at that time might possibly jeopardize future adventures (that could someday become great tales).

Well-Done Burger

When boys are growing up, they will usually eat about anything. However, one exception to this rule occurred at the country. Uncle John had taken Justin and Bernie to help do some outside cleanup around the cabin early on a Saturday morning. The plan was for them to work all morning and then he would feed them lunch and they could fish in the afternoon. He had a package of ground meat for hamburgers that he would cook in the frying pan on the old gas stove. The boys were working hard when John put the large patties in the skillet. There were several more chores that needed to be completed before lunch, and he knew it would be hopeless to get the boys back once they were turned loose at the pond. So he came out to supervise and help finish things up.

When all was done, Justin and Bernie went over to Uncle John's old Studebaker station wagon to get their fishing gear together while he finished preparing lunch. When the boys entered the cabin, it smelled sort of smoky. On the table were two plates with large hamburger buns and bottles of Coke. After the blessing, the boys, anticipating a juicy burger, took a big bite that tasted more like burnt air. They opened the bun, and there sat something that looked more like a tiny charcoal briquette—really small, about the size of a quarter. Uncle John apologetically said, "Hope you like it well-done." He had left the meat on the stove for almost forty-five minutes, which resulted in the burgers being burned to a crisp. Thus, the lunch turned out to be just a catsup and mustard sandwich with a Coke.

But disappointments do not linger long in the country. Thirty minutes later, these two adventurous boys were in the boat on the pond pursuing their coveted prey—the largemouth bass.

What's That Smell?

Because of his love for the outdoors that included hunting and fishing, Bernie wanted to learn more about mounting wild game. One of the sports magazines back then advertised a correspondence course on taxidermy. The fifteen-dollar fee bought six instruction manuals on mounting different types of wild animals, including birds and fishes. As each individual assignment was completed, another book would arrive. He signed up and had already completed three parts: a fish, a squirrel, and a small bird (cedar waxwing). He also tried a frog, but that didn't work out. Photos of the mounts that turned out well had been submitted. The next one was to be a large bird—maybe a duck, hawk, or goose. This was going to be more difficult to get than the smaller creatures. His mom suggested that he "stuff" a chicken, but that didn't seem quite appropriate.

Bernie drove up to the country in his dad's car to meet Justin and his dad for the day. Mr. Burgstiner listened to his plight to obtain a specimen for the next assignment and promised he would get what was needed. Ducks were out of season, hawks were on the endangered species list, and geese never stopped at the pond on their migratory flights. The boys were sitting on the bank when a rifle shot rang out. Mr. Burgstiner had spotted and shot a large bird that was perched high on a tree limb next to the pond. They paddled out and retrieved it. It was a big bird often observed around the pond called a water turkey. Ugly in appearance, it looks and acts sort of like a buzzard with a thin, snake-shaped head. This would not have been Bernie's first choice, but he had only a short time before the next assignment was due. Late in the afternoon, he drove back to Savannah with the prize in the trunk.

It was the middle of the summer, and the Browns didn't have air-conditioning at home. Bernie usually took a cool shower and slept with a window fan next to the bed. He was worn out from the day's activity and went straight to bed. About a week later, his dad came storming into his room and asked in a loud, highly irritated voice, "What is that stinking thing in the truck of my car?"

Bernie learned right then that there are times when no explanation is adequate, no excuse is acceptable, and even forgiveness will take some time. He had totally forgotten that the water turkey was in the trunk, and a week in the hot Savannah sunshine had made it very ripe—the aroma was unbelievably bad. He washed and washed and washed the car trunk and liner with limited success.

His dad traded cars often, due primarily to his poor driving habits that resulted in many dents. But he had a different reason to trade this time: a smelly trunk. It took a while, but he finally forgave his son. Needless to say, Bernie missed his deadline on this particular assignment and thus failed to finish the taxidermy course.

Guests in Our Bedroom

This was to be our greatest adventure ever. We had planned our summer trip to the country for the past six months. After school was out, we were going to stay four to five days. There were six of us boys who had worked mowing lawns and washing cars to make enough to cover our food and bait (worms and crickets). Bernie's family would be staying at the cabin, so we planned to camp down by the pond. In those days, there was an old boathouse that had a bunk room. It was really basic and rustic but better than sleeping on the ground or in a tent. We moved in with all our gear and supplies. On the first day, we almost wore ourselves out having fun. We explored and then fished a while and swam/bathed in the pond late in the afternoon. Our first meal that evening would probably be classified as snacks today. The full meals using our groceries would be on the days to come.

At dark, we had to settle in pretty quickly because we had only flashlights. Everyone was in his bunk and all the chatter had died down when Jerald jumped up and yelled, "Something's in my bed!" We surrounded the bunk, and surely enough, we could see something moving around inside the old, dilapidated mattress. A machete strike cut short the life of this intruder: a large rat. We all checked our own bunks to make certain there were no more varmints and eventually fell asleep from pure exhaustion. It wasn't a good start.

But the next morning, we put this behind us and headed over to Blue Springs. Our plan was to return to the pond and make lunch our big meal for the day. We had a great swim in the ice-cold water and were starving when we got back.

As we approached our bunk room, something seemed wrong; the door was wide open and we could hear loud grunting noises. Peering in, we could see furry images moving around, creatures that would soon reveal themselves. When they heard and saw us, a pack of wild hogs came charging out the door with grocery bags flying everywhere.

After regaining our wits, we inspected the crime scene. The vegetables were gone, all the meat from the ice chest had been tasted, the canned items were covered in teeth marks, and most soft drink bottles had been broken. An insurance adjuster would have labeled it a total loss.

In less than two days and just one night, we had our living quarters totally disrupted and all our food was gone. With so much commotion going on, Bernie's mom and dad came down to the pond to investigate. We were all invited up to eat lunch and then to spend the rest of our nights on the cabin's porch. Brother Brown, who was a preacher, must have had some connections. He and Mrs. Brown had a few "loaves and fishes" along with other food that kept us from starving for the balance of our stay.

While memories of an uneventful outing usually tend to fade, real adventures like this one are not easily forgotten. We are still telling this tale almost sixty years later.

Cut Off His Shirttail

Not all sports adventures at the country were related to fishing. Another opportunity involved hunting. There were coveys of quail along the fencerows, doves were constantly feeding in the fields, turkeys were roosting in the branches, and squirrels were scurrying through the woods. But deer were the most challenging of the wild game and also plentiful in the area.

Justin and Bernie were invited to go on their first deer hunt with Uncle John and some of the locals. They were placed in stands along with the others far enough apart for safety. On this particular hunt, dogs would drive the deer in the direction of the hunters. All were given instructions that were important to the success of the hunt.

For example, the hunter closest to where the deer crossed would take the shot. And most importantly, the dogs should be stopped at that point, or they might continue to trail and be lost.

There was some early excitement when a deer was shot by one of the older and more experienced hunters. Then everyone returned to his position for another drive. This time, Bernie could hear the dogs barking as they came closer and closer to his stand. All at once, he saw five deer coming across the field toward him. He was using a sixteen-gauge Winchester Model 12 shotgun that had been given to him by his uncle Bill Brown. It was loaded with buckshot.

Bernie moved to his left in order to be closer to the point where the deer would cross. Unfortunately, they were running very fast and the shotgun had only a short range. Nevertheless, he took a shot at the big buck that led the pack. Since they all continued on, it was an obvious miss. Bernie was disappointed yet still excited as the dogs crossed in hot pursuit of the prey.

All the hunters soon arrived, anticipating more venison to be shared with the group. Because of the missed shot, Bernie was informed that his shirttail would be cut off. This was a tradition practiced in those parts that symbolized failure. That was bad enough, but it got much worse. The dog owner then arrived and wanted to know where the dogs were—they were supposed to be stopped. Bernie's ears were scorched with words that can only come from someone so mad that no clean language is left in his vocabulary. Justin wanted to come to his friend's aid but concluded it was too late.

Then a miracle occurred. One of the other hunters said, "I can still hear the dogs," and started walking into the woods. The whole group followed for about three hundred yards and there lay a deer surrounded by the howling dogs. It was not the large buck leading the group but a smaller one that was trailing.

Bernie tucked his shirttail back in his pants and thought, *Deer hunting is not all that hard!* Sixty years later, he fondly remembers that day when he killed both his first and his last deer.

Early Adventures (1950s)
(Top and Middle) Justin and Bernie in the pond with friends; (Bottom) Bernie with Justin's dad

Chapter 3

Who Are the Bass Buddies?

THE EARLY ADVENTURES ENDED when Bernie's family moved from Savannah to Valdosta, and almost twenty years ensued before the two friends returned together to the country. This new phase of adventures started slowly with one or two visits per year by Justin and Bernie, the two original "buddies." Other friends were invited periodically, but soon Robert, Bernie's brother-in-law, became the permanent third party. Several years later, Earl, another brother-in-law, came on board to complete the team of four. Four was a good number since they took turns fishing together in twosomes.

In most years, the group made three or four trips during various seasons, which required different fishing strategies and techniques. Their skills as fishermen grew with experience and as new bait and tackle came on the scene. But more importantly, deep friendships that can only occur from spending a significant amount of quality time together developed. They, along with their wives, also took several trips together up to the mountains of North Carolina. The wives would never agree to go with their husbands on a fishing trip to the country, nor were they ever invited. It was designated as a "testosterone-only" zone.

Their team designation as Bass Buddies came into existence a few years later because of a particular incident. From time to time, each individual in the group would bring a small gift for the others. These included such things as caps, knives, new lures, and worms. One year, Bernie bought each of the group an outdoor-style shirt and had a friend (Jan Poland) embroider a striking bass with the insignia "Bass Buddies" above the pocket.

The group wore their shirts out to dinner in Statesboro one evening during a trip to the country. The Longhorn Steakhouse was packed that night. As they were waiting to be seated, the hostess gave them special attention. She came over and asked if they were fishermen (she probably meant professionals) and in a tournament. They answered, "Yes," honestly because they do fish, and they do compete with each other furiously for the most and biggest fish. When she inquired if this would be on TV, they modestly answered, "No, not this one." She proceeded to tell all the waiters and others that there were celebrities among them. Though no one asked for an autograph, they still savored all the attention.

Thus, the Bass Buddies were born. They include, from youngest to oldest, Earl, Justin, Bernie, and Robert.

As each of us shares a few individual experiences (tales) at the country, we shift into a first-person point of view. We are not authors by trade, so please forgive us if the language and grammar ain't perfect.

Enjoy!

Chapter 4

Earl

EARL BAGLEY IS A *retired teacher/coach and corporate sales executive. He and his wife, Betsy, live in Newnan, Georgia, and have two children and four grandchildren. He is the dishwasher for the team. He doesn't like to cook, so instead of taking his turn for this duty, he agreed to wash and clean up after every meal. The others are delighted with this arrangement.*

Tawny Port

On my initial visit to the country, I was informed that I would be the designated person to procure the "cough medicine" (otherwise known as tawny port) for the group. Not being a "cough medicine" connoisseur I enlisted the aid of Robert, one of my brothers-in-law. Since he was from a navy background, I was sure he would know where this medicine could be found.

We departed from the country, and as instructed, I proceed to the nearest cough-medicine store, otherwise known as a liquor store. Upon arrival at our destination, we got out of the truck, went in the store, and informed the clerk that we wanted a bottle of tawny port. He then gave us a look of bewilderment and confusion and informed us that he had not a clue what we were talking about. I then, tongue in cheek, commenced to inform him that it was an alcohol-based cough medicine that could only be sold in liquor stores. This led to further confusion and our hasty departure from the store.

Approximately four stores and three hours later, we returned to the cabin empty-handed. This news of our failure was greeted by a series of groans and muttering about Robert's and my inability to fulfill a simple task. After the great search for tawny port came up empty, I became the official POCM (procurement officer of cough medicine) for the group. After assuming this highly sensitive and important position, I immediately, upon arriving back at home, visited the wine cellar at my local Wal-Mart. I found a white zinfandel that the stock boy assured me had been aged at least fifteen to thirty minutes. Through the years, this cheap ($3.99 a bottle), sweet, fruity wine cured many a cough and became the group's favorite.

Backing the Trailer

There are sometime situations that are so funny but you have to be there to fully appreciate them. This is one of those times. At the end of this tale, I will ask you to close your eyes and picture what happened. Then maybe you can fully appreciate this story.

The road down to the pond at the country is very narrow and pocked with deep ruts. It ends at the dam with an area that is not much wider than the length of your vehicle and boat trailer combined. This small space necessitates strategic maneuvering of a manual nature to position both vehicle and trailer for backing up.

The "ramp" is an area about ten feet wide down a steep embankment that is wet and soggy. Extreme caution is taken so as not to have your vehicle slide down the ramp and into the lake.

Upon arriving at the ramp area, we always first unhook the trailer from the vehicle and pull it to one side. The vehicle is then oriented to the ramp and the trailer is reattached to it for backing down the ramp to launch the boat.

Backing a trailer requires a keen eye, cat-quick reflexes, and above all, competent and alert help. Now close your eyes and picture this scene.

As Robert is backing up his van, Bernie, Justin, and I offer guidance and directions—with a little ridicule thrown in. You can hear shouts of "Slower! Slower!" "Move to the right!" "Pull up! Pull up!" "Whoa! Whoa!" "Try again!" "Left! Left! Left!" *"What's wrong with you? Are you already into the cough medicine?"*

On this occasion, as we are all offering our assistance, I step back and realize that something is amiss. I shout to the rest of the group, "Houston, we have a problem!"

All chatter and movement cease as they look at me questioningly.

I answer, "Wouldn't it help if we had the trailer hooked to the van?"

Can you picture the hilarious scene and the looks on our faces as we fall to the ground in fits of laughter? Still makes me laugh every time I think about it!!

Is He Alive?

As our group has aged, we all have begun facing various health issues. One of these that has affected all of us to some degree is sleep apnea. Depending on the severity, our treatments range from taking a melatonin each night to using a CPAP breathing machine. Justin was the first to use the CPAP.

At the country, our normal sleeping arrangements include Robert and me sharing the guestroom with twin beds, Bernie on a foldout sleeper sofa in the den, and Justin sleeping in the main bedroom. At the time of this particular incident, Justin was using the breathing machine. Robert also had one but didn't feel the need to bring it. I don't think Bernie or I had ever seen one. Justin gave us all a little demonstration on its use.

Our second day there was a busy one. We had good luck, cleaned the fish, and showered before driving over to Statesboro for our night out at Longhorn Steakhouse. The short trip was a little traumatic because we struck a deer that crossed the road. Fortunately, neither the deer nor the car was damaged very much. We got back fairly late and went straight to bed; the next day's weather conditions looked perfect for fishing.

About 2:00 a.m., Bernie woke both Robert and me up, telling us to come out into the den. As soon as we were lucid, we could tell why he had called us. He said that he had been lying there for about thirty minutes listening to the gurgling sound coming from Justin's room. Evidently, the CPAP machine was not functioning properly, so he had glanced in and Justin seemed awfully still. Our unprofessional diagnosis was that he was not breathing and that was causing resistance to the mask covering his nose and mouth.

Bernie, who always has an opinion on what we ought to do, said, "Robert, you have one of those machines, so you go in there and check on Justin. He doesn't look like he's alive to me!" With great reluctance and much trepidation, Robert entered the room and poked Justin, who was lying on his stomach. He awoke immediately, saying, "What, what, what's going on?"

Evidently, the mask had slipped from its appropriate position and the machine was laboring, causing the unusual sound that we were hearing.

I don't remember how long it took me to go back to sleep that night or even if I did. We were just happy that our buddy was still alive.

No Water

Over the years, there have been many memorable moments spent at the country, fishing with my best friends—two of whom also happen to be my brothers-in-law. No matter what the circumstance, it has always been good clean fun—except for one unsavory occasion.

The cabin has been described previously and, as pointed out, offered all the amenities of home. On this one occasion as we arrived for our stay, we discovered the water pump had been rendered out of commission, probably by a lightning strike. No running water—no water of any kind! The only water available was what we brought with us for our consumption. As we took stock of our situation and inventoried our water, we had thirty twelve-ounce bottles to last us four days to be used for cooking and drinking only.

The first thing we figured we could do without was baths. Looking back, that was a bad mistake. After about two days of sitting under a south Georgia sun in a boat for eight to ten hours, to say we stank would be an understatement.

On the third day, I actually saw buzzards circling the cabin. I guess they figured there had to be something dead down there because it sure smelled like it! I absolutely refuse to discuss our toilet procedures but will say that they included implements of mass destruction and many excursions into the surrounding woods at all hours of the night.

On the fourth day, we departed for home with our olfactory nerves barely functioning after being assaulted by waves of indescribable odors. On the way home, it is my custom to stop at the same gas station to get gas and something to eat and drink. When I finished gassing up, I went inside, carefully avoiding contact with anyone. As my luck would have it, a mother came up the same aisle I was on. She stopped about five feet from me, and her little girl stood holding her nose. Then the mother grabbed her child and hurried her to the other side of the store. How embarrassing! I arrived home five hours later feeling like the *Peanuts* character Pigpen enveloped in a cocoon of dirt, dust, and stink. A shower never felt so good!

My Best Catch

There once were four guys who went fishing
To catch a big bass they were wishing.
Spent all day on the lake—
Not one bite—for Pete's sake!
So then they just went back to wishing.

It was probably an hour until sunset. Six hours on the lake with four or five bites. Frustration and desperation were my main thoughts. I had been skunked—the worst thing that can happen to a fisherman after a day on the lake.

I made my way back to the ramp area with plans to call it a day and go to the cabin to face the ridicule I knew was surely coming. During the day, I had tried almost every type of lure in my tackle box. Spinners, worms of every color (even pink), top-water poppers, and crank baits were used to no avail.

I then spied at the bottom of a pocket a red worm rigged with hooks and a propeller on the front that spun on retrieval. I was desperate, so I tied it on for a few last casts of the day.

Retrieving it on the fourth cast, the line suddenly tightened. I figured I had snagged on some submerged obstacle. All of a sudden, my line began to move rapidly sideways and I realized I had a bite. I leaned back and set the hook.

For maybe five to ten minutes, I battled with this fish. He finally surfaced, fishtailing out of the water in an effort to throw the hook. My mouth dropped open when I saw it and realized I had just caught a "wall hanger," which I later learned weighed about eleven pounds.

As the others arrived at the ramp to disembark, they began to call out the number of fish they had caught. I said nothing. When they had finished, I slowly retrieved my catch out of the live well and held it up with both hands and watched their jaws drop in amazement. In an instant, I went from being skunked to holding bragging rights—at least for that night.

What It Meant to Me

I have fished off and on for most of my life. I prefer the on times.

My father and I fished the coast of Georgia, and I enjoyed fishing with boyhood friends in the nearby lakes and rivers. I quit fishing when I left college except for the few times I would go with my father when I was home. After college I took up golf and it became my passion, and fishing vanished from my list of activities—until I eventually just never thought of it anymore.

Fifteen years or so later, my wife and I were talking about the special memories I have of fishing as a boy, and we decided we should give it a try. I went to the local Wal-Mart and purchased rods and reels, tackle, and lures for our first excursion to our local lake.

After this initial trip, my passion for fishing was reignited. This renewed interest resulted in the acquisition over the next few years of boats, motors, and everything that a fisherman could conceivably need or want.

Because of fishing—and especially our fishing trips to the country—I have become closer to Bernie, Robert, and Justin. They now have become not only my Bass Buddies but also my "Life Buddies."

While fishing, I often transcend the present and experience those same feelings I had in the past when I fished with family and friends. It was a much simpler time of life.

Fishing has allowed me to reflect on both good and bad times, and it has afforded me the opportunity to bond with nature. While in the country, watching the mist rise from the pond early in the morning or the sun setting late in the afternoon always makes me realize how beautiful this world is. At those times, I realize that God created this beauty out of His love for us. Fishing is a time of peace and relaxation. You could say that fishing is life's tranquilizer!

Chapter 5

Justin

JUSTIN BURGSTINER IS A retired telephone-company executive who lives in Savannah, Georgia. His wife, Carolyn, died in 2014. He has one child and two grandchildren. He is a before- and after-dinner speaker, the resident Jerry Clower of the group, and each time he repeats a story, it gets better.

Sinking the Boat: Our Conversion

On our first trip back to the country after growing up, we returned for relaxation. Bernie and I were excited to be young again, at least in our minds. We couldn't wait to go fishing. We went to the pond and got into the new ten-foot aluminum boat with bait of all kinds (worms, minnows, and crickets). We were going after them!

We were now "modern" because we had a large battery and a 1940s model electric motor that belonged to Bernie's father. Bernie provided me a football stadium seat that would not clamp to the boat bench as it should. The boat was not balanced because Bernie weighted about 180 pounds and I was 240 pounds. He had the giant battery in the back of the boat with him, so that helped some.

We were catching bream and redbreast right and left as we reached the first big inlet and decided to fish in there a while. All of a sudden, the stadium seat slipped backward in the boat toward Bernie and the battery. With 240 additional pounds in the back, you guessed it! The boat went down like the *Titanic!* Of course, we went under too.

Being good Methodists, this was a bit traumatic because we were more familiar with baptism by sprinkling than being dunked. Finally, we were able to touch bottom, which was not much comfort. There were hundreds of crickets everywhere, and the worms and minnows were all gone! We finally managed to get the boat, motor, battery, and most of our gear back to the shore. Thankfully, there were no alligators in the pond then, or I do believe we would have been walking on water for sure.

It was almost lunchtime before we could regroup. Without any bait, we were faced with a dilemma: we could drive back to Savannah for more or try something different. I had a package of plastic Tournament worms that I'd gotten in Valdosta. Since we didn't have the time, money, or desire to purchase more live bait, we ventured into a new world of fishing with artificial bait. This change also led us to use a variety of different baits, including not only plastic worms but also top-water lures, spinners, jigs, etc.

Our baptism by submersion was a life-changing experience. The most and largest fish that we all had ever caught resulted from switching from the old to the new way. God works in mysterious ways.

The Different Boats

Thinking back over the past sixty-plus years, I remember the different boats that we used. At first, we had a man-made wooden flat bottom boat with a couple of paddles. It was heavy and often leaked because the wood wasn't sealed real tight. We carried a bucket or large can to bail the water that had leaked in. A day out in this boat would absolutely wear you out.

Then one day Aunt Louise bought a lightweight aluminum one that was much easier to paddle and maneuver. With it, we could get to our "honey holes" quicker and quieter. We also used our first electric motors with this boat as well as cushions or stadium seats for seating comfort. Unfortunately, these could slide right out from under us, causing a number of incidences of capsizing and men overboard. I've already shared one of these tales with you.

Then we were introduced to a next-generation boat: a small, two-person, fiberglass pontoon that required the use of an electric motor. One time, my brother Henry and I, who are both pretty big guys, were fishing together in this boat. The weight caused the pontoons on both sides to be almost submerged. Our buddies would kid us unmercifully because it looked like we were just sitting on the water.

Robert was the first to bring a really comfortable boat to the country. It was a Basstender fiberglass model with an electric motor attached to a battery through an internal wiring system. The battery also powered an aeration well that kept the fish fresh. Additionally, he had a larger bass boat with a thirty-five-horsepower outboard motor. His decision to bring a sure'nough bass boat caused jealousy among our buddies. Initially, we all kissed up to Robert because each wanted to ride in his fancy, comfortable boat. Then Earl bought a similar one, and this was the beginning of a sequence of events that has no good explanation.

First, Robert decided to sell his larger boat, so Earl bought it and fixed it up. Then Robert decided to sell his smaller boat, so Bernie bought it. Earl then decided to sell the boat that he had fixed up, so Robert bought it back from him. Then Bernie decided he didn't need the one that he had bought from Robert, so he gave it to me. After all these transactions, we often didn't know whose boat we were fishing in. But you know what? It really didn't matter because we were Bass Buddies!

Stuck Like a Bullfrog

On one adventure, an alternate member of the Bass Buddies, Whit Byram, and I were fishing. Whit had to relieve himself, so we pulled the two-man boat up to the shore. After the mission was accomplished, we started to back up to continue fishing, but the boat wouldn't move; we were stuck on something. I put the motor in reverse, and we began rocking the boat back and forth. On one of those *forths*, Whit went overboard! To this day, I do not know how he bounced in and out of the water and landed on a stump so quickly. It might have something to do with the fact that earlier in the day we had come face-to-face with a big alligator. Somehow in all the commotion, my seat went overboard and Whit had me in a headlock with the motor going in reverse! I finally convinced him to let go of my head, so I could turn the motor off. Whit was able to get back in the boat, and we continued fishing. The moral of this story is to just *hold it!* (There are many versions of this particular tale but this is mine and I'm sticking to it!)

The Fly Sting

Here is one of those quick but lasting tales that have "stuck" with us. It's been told so many times that I'll need to fall back on my memory to make sure it's not been embellished or exaggerated too much. I'm the only one who can tell the true version because I was actually there to see it. On this occasion, Bernie and I were fishing in the pond. He found a fly—a small, artificial lure—on an overhanging limb and stuck it on his shirt to keep it. I knew he would forget about it, so I had a plan. When we arrived back at the dam after fishing for a few hours, I got out of the boat. Then I looked back at my friend and said, "Oh no, Bernie. What is that on your shirt?" He looked down and shouted, "Oh no! What is that?" and began trying to swat at the fly. With every swipe of his hand, the hook stuck him a little deeper, much like a bee sting. He fought it frantically for several moments before falling out of the boat into the pond. He finally gave up and remembered that this was the fly he had rescued from the limb and stuck on his shirt himself. I was laughing so hard that I could not catch my breath!

Of course, we all laugh every time we tell or hear the story. But sometimes, Bernie tries to get real philosophical and preachy about it to hide his embarrassment and humiliation. For example, he might point out that life would be awfully boring if we remembered everything and were perfect. He doesn't have to prove to us that he's not perfect; we already know it. We just enjoy having a tale that we can tell about him because he is always telling one about one of us. It will "stick" with him forever. Thankfully, Bernie can now laugh about it too.

My New Friend

My bedroom at the country is off by itself on the right side of the cabin. This is my room primarily because I'm pretty noisy at night—snore the loudest and use a breathing machine. Nobody ever wants to share a room with me, and to be honest, I don't want to share one with anyone anyway.

My first night's sleep on this trip was restless, which is not unusual for me. For some reason, I kept sensing that someone else was in the room; it must have been a bad dream. Then I heard a rustling sound and a squeaky noise. I have been around field mice all of my life, but I had never heard one squeak. This little buddy kept running under my bed and squeaking all night long, keeping me awake. I finally got up and caught a glimpse of the intruder running under the closet door. I got up and looked in the closet but could not see him. I turned the light on so I could take care of him with the broom. Eventually, he came back out, and I was armed. I hit everything in the room, except the mouse who had escaped into the pantry. For the next forty-five minutes, that mouse teased me by running from the closet to the pantry as if he was daring me to chase him. I gave up. For the next three nights, he "squeaked" me to sleep like a lullaby. Mouse, you win!

For some strange reason, there seemed to be a connection between this 260-pound human and that three-ounce field mouse. I figured out that the natural home for this little creature had probably been destroyed when the field next to the cabin had been harrowed for the spring planting season. He had sought refuge in my room.

My natural reaction to mice in the cabin is to put out some poison. However, in this case, I decided that maybe it was all right to share my room a few days with someone else, if he could handle my snoring. And I'm sure he missed his roommate after I left.

On our next trip to the country, we brought some of those pest-repellant devices that send out ultrasonic sound waves. This seemed to be a more humane way of telling these little critters to set up housekeeping in another place.

My Best Catch

My best catch is a fish that I did not catch at all. It is a beautiful nine-pound largemouth bass caught by my friend and buddy, Robert. Bernie had it mounted and presented to me in a special ceremony at his and Snookie's home at Lake Junaluska, North Carolina. I think they felt sorry for me since I had never had a "big catch." Since then, I have been fortunate to catch several large bass but have thrown them back. Maybe someone else will have the thrill of catching them. However, the best catches that I have made at the country are my true friends—these honorable, Christian men that I call "Bass Buddies."

What It Meant to Me

My adventures in the country began at a very early age. You see, I was born into the family. My family has owned this land, which is called Porter's Landing, since the late 1700s. My mother was raised on this property. I lived in Savannah but spent a lot of time in the country, which is about an hour from home. I was baptized at Mizpah Methodist Church, which was built with the help of my great grandfather Porter and his family. I stayed at the Porter house that was built in the 1830s many times. My first memories of Porter's Landing were in the late 1940s. We would go up there for barbecues and family reunions. My father, Frank Burgstiner, frequently took me to the country for hunting and fishing. He loved that place. He passed away at the young age of forty-three but had some of his happiest moments while at the country.

In 1954, Bernie and I began our adventures in the country. This friendship and tradition of going to that special place has now lasted over sixty years. As teenagers, we would help remove trees in the lake by ramming the boat into them and knocking them over. Luckily, we were not killed in the process. Later, we added two other members to the Bass Buddies: Robert and Earl. The times that we have shared on this "hallowed ground" are among my favorite memories.

Thankfully, my aunt Louise willed the country to my brother, cousins, and me. Today, I also enjoy going to the country with my grandsons and son-in-law. It is now one of their favorite places to hunt and fish as well. When you enter Porter's Landing, you feel a wonderful peace. I feel a connection with my past and future at the same time. We are blessed that God has given us such a special place to enjoy His creations.

Chapter 6

Bernie

BERNIE BROWN IS A retired health-care executive and author who lives in Marietta, Georgia, with his wife, Snookie. They have three children and eight grandchildren. He is the group's counselor who starts most conversations with "Let me tell you what you ought to do!" Unfortunately, from his point of view, most of this excellent advice is discounted.

An Explosive Dinner

One of my good professional friends was the administrator of the hospital in Statesboro. I had been hunting and fishing with Waymon Reece several times; we enjoyed a mutual appreciation for the outdoors. Waymon's friend Dr. Sam Tillman owned a beautiful farm in Millen, which was about forty-five minutes from the country. I also became acquainted with Dr. Tillman, who invited us to come over to his place to fish from time to time. Waymon was a great cook. He would grill fantastic meals for large groups, at times even serving all the Auburn fans from Statesboro at that school's football games. On several occasions when we drove over to fish at the farm, he prepared unbelievable dinners for us.

Late in the afternoon on one such occasion, it began to rain. So we retreated into an old farmhouse on the property and sat around one of those kitchen tables that you find in antique shops. There was an old stove that was partly functional; its oven didn't work. This was one of those evenings that we all were looking forward to—a gourmet meal produced by our talented host. The main course was to be some kind of catfish casserole, which if history repeated itself would melt in our mouths and we would want the recipe to impress our wives. I even remember bragging back home about the great chef that prepares meals for us on some of our fishing trips. He had already mixed up a wonderful salad, and we could see a large bowl of bread pudding on the counter for desert. Homemade sweet iced tea was our beverage. It doesn't get any better than this.

With no oven available, Waymon took the glass casserole dish out of his cooler and placed it on the largest burner on top of the stove to heat it. We all began reliving our day out on the lake. We had caught several bass in the four- to five-pound range and had some real excitement landing a couple of gars. We always had good luck at Dr. Tillman's place, or as we put it, "Our outstanding fishing skills were quite apparent when fishing there!"

Then all of a sudden, our conversation and fellowship was interrupted by a loud explosion. Glass and casserole components littered the entire kitchen. Fortunately, none of us were facing the stove. We all had an opinion on what happen, but my theory is as good as any. Because the dish was cold and the stove's burner was hot, a catalytic explosive reaction occurred, causing the container with its content to be propelled in an outward direction, thus removing from the night's menu the main dish.

We all helped with the cleanup effort and sat down again. After reassuring Waymon that he would be retained as our chief chef, we enjoyed a wonderful salad and dessert meal. Plus we felt proud that we were vegetarians for one night, and a great new tale was born. Waymon died several years ago; Genelda, his wife, gave us permission to share this with you.

Sons-in-Law

Usually when one in our group can't go to the country, we invite an alternate so we will have four. This particular time, only Justin and I were going so we needed two substitutes. We decided to invite our sons-in-law who already knew about each other but had never met. My daughter Amanda's husband, Brad, was my guest. Brad is one of a kind—born and raised in south Georgia with the accent and personality that give away his roots. I really like this because I grew up in that area too. He's one of the most educated in our family with an engineering degree from Georgia Tech, an MBA from Georgia State, and a theology degree from Southern (Baptist) Seminary in Louisville, Kentucky.

It was wintertime and pretty cold for the country. We had fished and hunted and were tired after the long first day. Brad and I shared the guest room with twin beds. When I sleep at night, I turn the heat way down and open the windows for fresh air. We also have a tradition of drinking a small glass of tawny port each evening. In light of Brad's strict Baptist upbringing, he was hesitant to join in the nightcap, but because he was with his father-in-law, I guess he felt obligated to comply.

The next morning, he checked in with Amanda, and I could hear part of the conversation. She had asked, "How's it going?" Brad told about the day and then said, "We had an interesting night. Even though it was thirtysomething degrees, your dad left the windows open. But I was okay in my warm sleeping bag, and we had some 'cough medicine' before we turned in that really helped." The next night he asked for his "cough medicine" before bedtime.

A few months later, we were visiting Brad and Amanda in Kentucky to help with the renovation of their attic. After the first workday, the kids were already in bed and we were just about ready to retire ourselves when Brad went into the kitchen. He came out with two juice glasses and said, "Why don't we have some 'cough medicine' before going to bed?"

It's Going To Be All Right

As mentioned earlier, visiting with Aunt Louise, E.L., and Teeny Cowart at the country was always a blessing and a highlight while there. I could tell many stories about each of these dear friends, but let me share something very special about E.L. He was a banker by profession and worked for Mr. Mills B. Lane, founder of the C&S Bank, which later through various mergers and consolidations became Bank of America. He was probably the most successful businessman that I knew personally at that time. Despite his lofty status, his demeanor was always kind, humble, and even-tempered. Later in life, I viewed him as one of my role models in the business world.

I will never forget receiving a phone call from my mom telling me that E.L. had suffered a massive stroke only a few days after she had returned from a trip with him and his wife, Teeny. It was touch and go for weeks, but he survived. This was followed by months of therapy. We visited several times during the rehabilitation period and could see gradual progress as he became mobile and mentally aware of things. He even improved enough to be able to return to their home in the country. I think this was one of the goals that motivated him to keep going. For the rest of his life, he would walk with a noticeable limp and weakness on one side like many stroke victims.

But there was another repercussion. E.L. had lost his ability to talk. Later, we would observe him listening and understanding everything that was said. Teeny would often answer for him, and at times, he would nod his head in response to questions. I was not entirely accurate in saying that he had lost total ability to speak. There was one phrase that he could say clearly and meaningfully. When we arrived for a visit, when we shared things that were going on in our lives, when we were getting ready to go down to the pond to fish, once when we were changing a tire, and on many other appropriate occasions, he would share his entire vocabulary with us in this phrase.

Many times after my visits to the country, I would wonder what it would be like to be unable to talk. Or if given just a few words to say, what I would want them to be. I would ask God to please give me the same words he gave my role model, E.L. Cowart. It always brings a smile to my face when I remember this great man saying to us, "Boy, boy, boy, it's going to be all right."

The Pécan

There is a nut that grows plentifully in south Georgia called the pecan. Actually, it is one of the region's major crops. Pecans are used in all types of recipes, including salads, baked breads, entrees, and desserts. This little nut can be pronounced a couple of ways: *pa-kon* or *pé-can*. I remember someone trying to clarify the difference in the two pronunciations. He indicated that *pa-kons,* which sounds much more sophisticated, come from trees in the front yard while *pé-cans,* a less refined term, refers to nuts from trees in the backyard. That made a lot of sense to me. This has been a mild bone of contention between my wife and me. She uses the first pronunciation, which is the wrong one, and I call it by the second. When this comes up, Snookie always counters by claiming, "Your pronunciation refers to what you carry in the boat!" I agree with her in part; when I'm out in a boat for an extended period of time, there often is a need for a can like that. This brings to mind a funny incident that occurred on a trip to the country. For some reason, so many of my tales originate from those times when Justin is in the boat. Incidentally, we usually carry such a can with us, a plastic one that came home from someone's hospital visit. There they called it a "urinal."

After a good breakfast with a couple of cups of coffee, we headed out in our boat. It was hot that morning, so I drank a can of root beer. The fish were active, and we were focused on our objective: catching. Under circumstances like this, bodily functions are generally ignored until nature's call reaches a crescendo. I was in the back operating the motor, and Justin was up front facing forward. "Where is the can?" I shouted.

He threw it back to me. The process of using the can in the boat involves pouring the contents out into the pond and then rinsing it out with pond water for the next use. At that point, my mischievous side kicked in. After rinsing, I filled it up with pond water and pretended that I still needed relief. I filled and emptied the container about five or six more times. Justin took the bait, grasping the severity of the situation and exclaimed, "My gosh! Bernie, how much did you drink this morning?"

I have to be careful when joking with Justin; he's a pretty big guy and with minimum provocation has been known to turn a boat over. My measured response to his question was "I think I'm finished now." I had to fess up later to my deception when he started telling everyone that I surely must have a kidney infection.

How Much Grits?

Grits is a southern favorite and is one of the side dishes that we often had on our trips to the country. I'm usually the one who brought and prepared grits for breakfast with eggs and bacon and even with fish for supper. After all those years, I finally became comfortable with the right amount to cook for our group. This wasn't always true, as is evident in a couple of experiences that called into question just how much grits is enough. Let me share them with you.

On a father-son trip to the country back in the 1950s, my father was responsible for one of the meals for the group of eight. If you had known my dad, you would be well aware that something bad was going to happen when he was in the kitchen. His involvement there at home largely amounted to finding his chair at the kitchen table, saying the blessing, and eating more than anyone else. His charge during this trip was to prepare a country-style breakfast of eggs, bacon, toast, and grits.

The amount of everything except the grits seemed to be obvious, but Dad evidently wasn't certain how much of it to cook. So to be on the safe side and make certain that we had enough, he decided to cook a cup for each of us for a total of eight cups. To put this in perspective, Snookie cooks a half of a cup for the two of us, and we usually have a little left over. You can't imagine how much grits eight cups will produce. Every pot and container in the cabin was full by the time it was all done. In addition to serving the guests, most of the wild life in the vicinity also had grits for breakfast that morning.

From the other side of the spectrum on how much grits to prepare came a story that Earl shared with us. When he was in sales for a large light-fixture company, he often hosted folks from all over the country. On one occasion, he was taking one of his Yankee customers out for a good southern breakfast. The waiter at the restaurant asked Earl's guest if he would like some grits. The alien to this part of the country thought a minute and answered, "I believe I'll try it. Could you just bring me one?"

Reading all this, perhaps you can see why I initially had trouble deciding just how much grits to cook for the four of us on our trips. Then I discovered something astounding. All I had to do was read the directions on the side of the box of grits. I must admit that is hard for us men to do, sorta like stopping to ask for directions on the road when we are hopelessly lost. Interestingly, after this experience, we also discovered that most of the fishing gear and tackle we used also came with instructions. I think we all became better fishermen when we finally learned that it's all right to admit that we don't know everything.

Best Catch

My best catch is quite unusual. Let me explain.

It was in the early 1980s. Justin and I were fishing together using a new plastic worm that looked very much like a little snake. Actually, it was called "moccasin" because the coloring was very similar to the water moccasins native to the pond. We had caught a couple of nice bass and were excited about this new discovery. Justin cast into a small inlet and had a light strike, but the fish turned loose before he could set the hook. As we moved along, I cast in the same general area. My bait never hit the bottom but was immediately taken, dragging the line out toward the middle of the pond. I set the hook as hard as I could and then heard a big splash on the other side of the boat. The fish had swum under the boat and begun to pull us out from shore.

The next few minutes, which seemed like an hour, were occupied with my efforts to bring the monster in without breaking a line or allowing it to carry us into the overhanging bushes or stumps out in the channel. Finally, it was close to the boat and I was able to direct it into the net that Justin held. Without question, it was the biggest fish that I had ever caught. We left it in the net and went directly to shore. A scale on the porch of the cabin confirmed that I had caught a lunker. It weighed between eleven and twelve pounds, so I rounded it off to the higher. I had it mounted and exhibited proudly on our den wall.

I began by saying my tale was "unusual," and you might be wondering what is so unusual about this. The answer lies in the rest of the story. Almost twenty years later, Justin and I were again fishing together and were about twenty feet from the spot where my trophy was caught. Every time we approached that area, fond memories returned. This time I was using a new pumpkin seed worm. The line tightened, and I could tell that a fish was taking it to the deep waters. I set the hook, and the tug-of-war began.

It was like a repeat performance of a wonderful play. The actors, the dialogue, the climax, and the curtain call were the same. This large fish weighed between ten and eleven pounds, and once again, I rounded it off to the higher. I decide to have it mounted together with my first. The taxidermist refurbished the original one and used a large piece of driftwood as the base for the pair.

I share this tale every time a visitor views the two monster largemouths on the den wall. And I always make the point that history can repeat itself, and lightning can strike twice at the same spot. Truth can be stranger than fiction. So now you can understand why I contend this is so unusual: my best catches spanned a twenty-year period.

What It Meant to Me

Everyone probably has places that are special to him or her. I have a lot of these, but some rank above the others. The country is high on that list. When asked why, the following thoughts immediately come to mind.

First, when traveling there for a visit, my mind drops into a slower gear. As we turn off the paved onto the dirt road, my blood pressure and pulse rate seem to drop. When the gate opens, I feel welcome. The fields and the forest that we pass bring a sense of calmness; the cabin signifies rest from my worries; the pond conjures up anticipation of a catch; the river with its fast current brings excitement. In short, the country is a peaceful place.

Second, the people whose paths I crossed there have had a tremendous influence on my life. They include some of my best and longest friendships. They span three generations. Some of these are lifelong friends, some are professional colleagues, some are family members, others are new and old acquaintances, and a few are no longer with us. The country folks are an awesome clan of loving people, and I'm so glad that I have been privileged to be a part of it.

Third, as I become reacquainted with this place each time I visit, I cannot help but marvel at the beauty, serenity, and scope of this land with its vegetation, its cultivation, its reservoirs, and its clear skies that play host to all sort of creatures: animals, birds, fish, and us humans. Then my mind searches for answers to questions like who could have made such a place. My only conclusion is a divine Creator had something to do with it.

In the truest sense, this place is a transforming sanctuary for mind, body, and soul. I thank God for this wonderful blessing called "the country" that will forever hold a special place in my heart.

Chapter 7

Robert

ROBERT TAYLOR IS A retired engineer who lives in Nashville, Tennessee, with his wife, Suzanne. They have three children and nine grandchildren. He is an accident getting ready to happen; more tales have originated with Robert's activities than with any of the others.

The Car Is Locked

Even though I'm the oldest and smartest of the four Bass Buddies, I probably would win the prize of being the most forgetful. There are numerous examples of this, but my most notorious one occurred on a trip to the country. Bernie was riding with me, and we arrived much earlier than the others, with plans to get in an afternoon of fishing before supper. I had pulled my boat all the way from Nashville. It's always a little tricky to back the trailer down the slippery dirt ramp, but I did my usually good job positioning it so it could slide safely into the water. I released the boat from the winch and lowered it as Bernie controlled the rope attached to the bow—another perfect launch.

I turned around to pull the van and trailer back from the edge and noticed that the rear door was closed. When I tried to open the front door on the driver's side, I found it locked, and so were all the others. That was bad enough, but then I realized that the motor was still running. Through the window, I could see the key still in the ignition. I have to give Bernie credit; he didn't lose it when I explained that I had locked us out of the vehicle while it was still running. We were probably at least five miles from any other humans.

We tried to approach this like any two smart-thinking adults. After discounting about every different option that we could think of, I know that we both were praying privately for some kind of miracle. Eventually, we decided to walk up the hill to the cabin, though we had no key to get in. Fortunately, the small utility shed was unlocked. There we found an old clothes hanger that we straightened out. Back at the van, we discovered a slightly opened window so with the hanger, we were able to snake it down to press the window switch. That lowered the window, allowing us to reach in and open the door. All this might sound innovative and even brilliant, but in reality, it took about three hours. As we were pulling up the van and trailer, our other buddies arrived and asked how many we had caught. It was probably just as much fun sharing this tale with them as showing them a nice string of fish.

And you know there must be something to prayer. The shed was unlocked, a clothes hanger was available, the van's window was slightly cracked, and the car was still running, allowing us to open the window with the hanger. Best of all, a great tale was born.

A Light Supper

When we started going back to the country, Aunt Louise, E.L., and Teeny were still living there. They were always so hospitable, even to the point of often preparing meals for us. This seemed like somewhat of an imposition on our part, so we decided that we should cook for them some of the time. Here was our first attempt at a meal. It was to be supper for us all, sort of a one-dish meal that we had prepared several times before for ourselves. Individual servings of vegetables and chicken were seasoned and wrapped in tin (aluminum) foil to be cooked slowly at two hundred degrees in the oven for about five to six hours. While the guys were fishing in the afternoon, those remaining at the cabin were told to just let it cook until suppertime. A couple of times during the afternoon, Aunt Louise had mentioned to Teeny that it sure smelled like it was about done. But she was reminded that the boys had left "Do not disturb" instructions.

When everyone had returned and the time arrived for the evening meal, we opened the oven door and handed each person a serving. Aunt Louise commented, "This seems awfully light."

As the foil was opened, a terrible discovery was made; all that remained in each serving was a pile of black ashes. She was right; it was a "light supper." We were flabbergasted and couldn't imagine what had happened. Then a check of the oven revealed the cause. The knob used to set the temperature was confusing. It had been erroneously set at four hundred rather than two hundred degrees. Incidentally, this stove had been in the cabin for at least forty years.

Despite the catastrophe, no one starved because Aunt Louise and Teeny came to the rescue with a few things from their pantries and freezers. Next time maybe we can do better as the community chefs.

And there was another surprise—this time, a pleasant one. Bernie's birthday was coming up the next week, and Teeny had secretly prepared the dessert that Snookie always cooks for him each year instead of a birthday cake: rice pudding.

It is interesting to note that the well-done burgers cooked by Uncle John thirty-five years earlier and this "light supper" had two things in common. First, the two meals were cooked on the same stove, and second, in both cases, disappointments in the country did not linger long.

The Ugly Lure

From time to time, we have a substitute or alternate to join us when a member of the team can't come to the country. This incident occurred when we had a guest. Jerald had been with us before, but this was the first time that he and I had fished together. I have always felt that one of my strengths has been knowledge of the latest tackle. I'm often the one that identifies and procures a new lure or worm that might work for us.

When we were getting into the boat, I noticed that Jerald's rods and tackle box looked pretty dated. I was handling the motor in the back and he was sitting up front, so I could easily observe not only his gear but also his technique. When we start out from the dam, we usually try different baits and patterns to see what works best on that particular day. He was trying some things that I didn't recognize, but at that time, I hadn't known him long enough to offer advice. As I recall, I caught a few medium-size bass and he didn't have a strike during the first couple of hours.

We were heading back toward the dam when he pulled out a very large lure and tied it on his line. I asked him, "What is that?"

I'm not sure he gave it a name, but in my mind, it was not the right thing to use in the pond. To me, it was just big and ugly. But he proceeded to cast it out in the middle near one of the stumps. (I've never caught anything out in the middle; it's best to fish near the shoreline with all the overhanging trees and bushes.) He was drinking a root beer, so he laid his rod and reel down for a couple of minutes. He then picked it back up and started to reel in that monstrosity of a lure that just seemed to cause a lot of ripples in the water. On about the third turn of the reel's handle, an explosion occurred where the bait was. I could hear the reel surrendering line as Jerald attempted to gain control of the battle.

Sometime later, I held the net in amazement as he prevailed and the trophy largemouth, destined to hang on the wall, came on board.

After things settled, I took a closer look at the bait he was using. It was a giant *hula poppa* that is typically used in the evening or night. It is known for the noise it creates and, in my opinion, is one of the ugliest of all lures. But what do I know?

Trolling for Bream

Sometimes when you are fishing, all your well-laid plans just don't work out. Often in such cases, the result is an unsuccessful day on the pond and at worst being skunked. However, every once in a while, an unplanned turn of events will change the course of things. Let me tell you what I mean.

I was fishing with Justin, and Bernie and Earl were together. None of us were doing much, as we had tried just about everything in our tackle boxes to attract the bass. We were coming out of a cove when a nice fish struck a small spinner bait out in the open water. He went straight down, unlike a bass that usually comes to the surface and tries to dislodge the lure. When I landed it, as suspected, I had a bream—a very large one. We hardly ever fish for bream because in our minds bass are the ultimate freshwater prize. We do catch a few of them from time to time, but it's usually unintentional as we are pursuing bass.

After taking a look at that fish, however, both Justin and I had a mindset change. We started to cast the small spinners and caught a couple of more nice bream. As we were leaving the cove and heading back toward the dam, we let our baited lines trail the boat. This is called trolling. Almost immediately, we both hung two more nice ones. As we continued, more strikes occurred. We reached the dam and decided to troll up the opposite side of the pond. The same thing happened on that side; our stringer of large bream lengthened. We followed our original route up and down each side a few more times with similar success.

Bernie and Earl rounded the curve in their boat and watched as we continuously moved around. This led to a conversation that went something like this:

Them: "What are you guys doing?"

Us: "We are trolling!"

Them: "You can't troll in the pond; there are too many stumps!"

Us: "You do it your way, and we'll do it our way. How many have you caught?"

Them: "None, but we've had a couple of strikes. You all caught any?"

Us: "Just a few!" (We raised our stringer with about two dozen large bream.)

Them: "What are you fishing with?"

Interestingly, the rest of the afternoon they followed behind us with their baits trailing. The end result was the largest and most bream any of us had ever caught. Now, every time the bass aren't biting, you can usually find us trolling for bream. And on those days, maybe we should call ourselves "bream buddies."

Best Catch

My best catches both occurred in the pond at the country. Two twelve-pound bass are proudly displayed in the entry hall of my home. They were caught at different times, but I had them mounted together. Up here in Tennessee, bass don't grow this big, so they are observed with amazement and envy by neighbors who visit us. I must admit that many of my fishing skills were developed and honed at the country, where I have been fishing for over fifty years. These skills have also served me well at other locations. In this regard, let me share with you my most unusual catch, which occurred back home in a lake in our subdivision.

The lake had been stocked with tilapia, bream, and bass, which can be caught with the same techniques used at the country. It was summer and the fish had finished spawning and could be observed moving around in schools. From the bank, I could cast close to them with a gig or small spinner. I had caught a couple of small bream, when the gig was struck by a fish that headed deep and toward the middle of the lake. It was obvious that I had a good fish; the drag began to give line on the light spinning reel. At first, I suspected it was a largemouth, but it didn't come to the surface, and the aggressive strike wasn't like a bream or tilapia either.

I took my time, not wanting to break a line, and I didn't have a landing net with me. The fish wore out before I did, and I began bringing it to shore. My initial view was of a large redbreast that indicated a variety of sunfish similar to bream. If that was the case, it certainly would be a lake or a state or maybe even a world record.

I dragged the big fish up on shore and immediately ruled out my first impression. If it wasn't a redbreast, what was it? I handled it carefully because it appeared to weigh at least four pounds and had a mouthful of sharp teeth.

After carrying it home and conducting some research, the mystery fish was identified. I probably hold the record for the largest piranha ever caught in the state of Tennessee. The presumption was that years earlier someone had released it and possibly others that had outgrown a home aquarium. This was also a first for the mounting taxidermist who did a wonderful job on this beautiful and unique catch that hangs beside my two giant bass.

By the way, you should hear what my neighbors say now when viewing my trophies on the wall! Oh, and once the word got out, there was no worry about anyone sneaking into the lake to swim.

What It Meant to Me

Fishing always played an important part in my life. My father was an excellent fisherman; he even constructed the boat that we often used in the gulf. It was made of wood, had Styrofoam in the infrastructure to promote floatation and safety, and had two fifty-horsepower outboards on the rear. It was an engineering marvel that was ahead of its time. Growing up, I fished in saltwater, in local lakes, and even in streams. I can remember going down the road from our home to a creek and catching a mess of bream that my mother fried for our supper. This wonderful pastime has always been a passion for me and my two brothers, Max and Pat.

After college, I was in the navy for a tour of duty and then became busy launching an engineering career. During that period, there was less time and opportunity to devote to extracurricular

Adventures of the Bass Buddies

activities, including my favorite sport: fishing. And as a result, I missed regular fishing outings.

The first time that I visited the country was a couple of years after Suzanne and I were married over fifty years ago. And a few years later, I became one of the original Bass Buddies, joining Justin and Bernie. Justin and I became good friends, and Bernie is Suzanne's brother, thus my brother-in-law. Earl, another brother-in-law, joined us a few years later to complete the regular foursome.

The return to regular fishing trips brought back memories of my childhood—particularly the thrill of catching a big one, the disappointment of missing a big one, and the dream of catching an even bigger one. But more importantly, fishing to me was a "family affair," and in a sense a new family of brothers began to emerge. After fishing with a group of guys for over fifty years, one of two things happens. You either get tired of them or you get used to them. I guess that I just got used to them, because I always looked forward to our next trip together and now cherish the memories of past adventures with my brothers.

The Bass Buddies making a fashion statement.

Chapter 8

The Alternates

FROM TIME TO TIME, before the four-person team was set, and also later when a member of the group couldn't come on a trip, others were invited to join us. We always enjoyed the various guests who added a new dimension to our fun and fellowship and expanded the scope of our tales. Usually, a story or two would grow out of every visit by an alternate. In the early days, Justin and Bernie had a host of teenage buddies along for weekends and during the summer. Many of these adventures and escapades cannot be recorded on grounds they might be incriminating. Some of you can probably identify with this. Also, it would be difficult now to remember all those who came so long ago.

So let's concentrate on the alternates or substitutes who joined us during the later years. We thought you might enjoy a few thoughts and comments from some of them about their experiences.

John Bowling
(Retired Health-Care Executive)

At first it was all about the catching—who could catch the biggest fish and who could catch the most fish. Then as we all grew a little older, it became less about the catching and more about the *fishing*. Sleep in a little later, drink another cup of coffee, enjoy a little more conversation, and amble, not race, down to the pond. Then it became more about the relationships; that's where my most cherished memories of "the country" now reside.

Since most of our stories are told in other parts of this book, I want to share a few reflections about the cast of characters as I see them. Aunt Louise was the gracious lady who owned the property and truly seemed to enjoy having "the boys" come for a visit. Justin was her nephew and our access to an invitation to fish. He was my favorite boat partner because entertainment was his specialty.

Bernie was my longtime friend, boss, and health-care colleague. He was the last holdout in moving from the catching to fishing stage, the most intense about getting us moving in the morning toward catching a big one!

Robert was the tackle king, and I don't mean football! He had as much fun getting ready to fish as he did actually fishing—he always had the latest in lures. Pink bubblegum plastic worms were his claim to fame, and though we were all snickering at first, we were right in there with him once his success was evident.

Richard was another hospital colleague and pal who was less about the catching or fishing and more about the conversation. He had a sincere interest in all members of the cast and was a great listener.

E.L. and Teeny had moved onto the property at the invitation of Aunt Louise. E.L. had recently retired from C&S Bank and Teeny was one of those ladies who served as our second mother while we were there. She housed us, cooked for us, and set for us a beautiful example of Christian servanthood.

Now that you've met the cast (at least the ones I knew), perhaps the stories you have just read will make more sense.

Bucky Smith
(Retired Printing-Company Executive)

It was a Sunday, and Bernie and I had just arrived after the long drive from Marietta. We threw our gear into the cabin and then headed for the pond for a few hours of fishing before dark. It was then that Bernie told me that fishing on Sunday was against Aunt Louise's religion. She was very adamant about this, and no one wanted to get on her wrong side. However, knowing that she would not be at the cabin until the next day, we decided that if we caught anything, we would throw it back. He did not have to persuade me to wet a line for a few hours before dinner.

At my first view of the pond, I immediately thought, *That's sally water*. You might ask, "What is a sally?" More specifically, a yellow sally is a three-part lure comprised of a weighted single hook with a bright yellow feather, a number 4 Hildebrandt spinner, and a number 11 Uncle Josh pork frog on the hook. The advantage of this rig is that it can be fished in heavy structure. The depth of the lure can be controlled by the speed of the retrieve. You can bring it across the top of the water, bring it across logs, or slow the retrieve and it will go just under the surface. Either way, the yellow sally is one of the best big-bass lures I've ever seen. It was a favorite of Georgia Tech coach Bobby Dodd, himself a prolific bass fisherman. It is deadly.

We had not been in the water long when I made a cast parallel to the shoreline of hanging tree branches, most of them dipping right into the water. As I was bringing it back just a few inches under the surface, the water suddenly exploded. Setting the hook hard, the rod almost came out of my hand. I knew she was a big one.

After what seemed like an eternity, Bernie carefully slipped the net beneath the big fish. While I had caught big bass before, the thrill was again exhilarating; my heart was pounding.

Once safely in the boat, the reality of it being Sunday set in: we were not supposed to fish on Sunday. I love Bernie, but I'll be doggone if I was going to throw this fish back. Truthfully, if he had insisted, I would have done so. What were we to do? A true fisherman cannot keep such a prize catch a secret. So we packed this monster bass in a chest full of ice.

The next day, after the morning swing around the pond, we pulled the big bass out to show it off, pretending it had just been caught, along with some other ones. It was stiff as a board with eyes all glazed over, and I wasn't sure if Aunt Louise realized that it was not a freshly caught one. We didn't keep it out long, quickly placing it back in the ice chest.

I was blessed to travel to the country several times over the years. Each visit would bring forth stories of yesteryear, great food, and even sweeter fellowship. Fishermen love to catch fish, especially big ones, but the real joy of such trips is the fellowship. My thanks for letting me be part of the Bass Buddies. Incidentally, that big bass hangs on my wall today.

Richard Hubbard
(Retired Health-Care Executive)

The first thing that comes to mind about "the country" is that it is *really* in the country. Can't say I have ever spent time in a quieter, more serene, more remote, and more beautiful place. I still remember the cabin where we stayed, and I might also mention that there were a couple of nights when we were not the only occupants. A few woodland creatures joined us. I also recall being there two or three days without seeing or hearing a single vehicle pass on the dirt road in front of the house. The only human-generated noise was from the occasional motorboat on the Savannah River, which was behind and down the hill from the cabin. We were almost in South Carolina!

When everyone arrived, the process of getting our boats down to the pond could present challenges, but it always worked out so we could launch them from the dam. My first sight of the pond will always be a fond memory for me. It had to be the "fishiest" pond I had ever seen, but it also might qualify as the "snakiest" pond I had ever seen. Next came the decision of who would be in whose boat. It seems to me that the only requirement was that Justin liked to be in a boat where he could get his nap in! He always had his rifle, and sometimes if the fish weren't biting, we would do a little target practice shooting turtles off logs. We even caught fish, but I don't remember us filling up our stringer. Could be the better fishermen were always in the other boat. At the end of day, we headed back up the hill to the cabin and Chef Justin went to work on a low country boil. We always ate well, after which we and our little *creatures* would turn in.

One experience that I especially remember was the time I had to leave a day early and got a little lost trying to find my way back to the interstate highway. Finally, I stopped at a crossroads where an elderly gentleman was standing in front of a little store. I asked directions. He pointed straight ahead and said, "Just keep agoing straight; it's paved road all the way!" I thanked him and moved on, grinning to myself because it had been years since directions had included the safety of a paved road. Yes, we were in the country, and it was great!

Whit Byram
(Ordained United Methodist Minister)

Memories of the Country
There's a peaceful spot where I love to be;
For thirty-seven years, I've called that place "the country."
A cabin and pond provided good times to seize;
All were welcome to come by the gracious Aunt Louise.

Turning on the Clyo-Kildare Road meant we were almost there;
Leaving thoughts of school and work behind, we hadn't a care.
Just being together with family and friends was a treat;
Fishing and resting were done, with plenty of good things to eat.

There was that time the hook went through Bill's arm;
We made it back to the Cowarts' before too much harm.
EL knew just what to do, for he was truly a saint,
And he was doing quite well, before he got faint.

We almost lost Justin, the day he fell out of the boat;
With the motor in reverse, it was a good thing he could float.

Unwrapped from the log and wet from his head to his toes,
We still made it back down, for the afternoon mosquitoes.

Memories are a gift from the God of heaven and earth,
 A gift that is priceless with immeasurable worth.
 Buddies share a bond, a connection without end,
 A true blessing from the One who calls us his friend.

That beautiful piece of property became a sacred space;
Both refuge and retreat were found, pausing life's hectic pace.
 But life doesn't stay paused for long, that much is true;
  So I'm grateful for good friends and
  gatherings that help see us through.

Ryon Rambo
(Owner of Landscaping Service)

When I think of the country, I think of relaxation. I have nothing but wonderful memories of fishing, hunting, and shooting skeet there. One late afternoon, Justin (Poppy) and I were fishing in the pond. It was getting dark so I hinted to Poppy several times that maybe we needed to head back to the shore. If you know Poppy, then you know it is sometimes difficult to get him to leave. Pop said, "No, we have plenty of time to get out before it is too dark."

There are numerous stumps in the pond, and just as we were heading to the shore, we got caught on one. We rocked back and forth and pushed with the paddle but could not get loose. It kept getting darker and darker. Taking a break from rocking and pushing with the paddle, I noticed two eyes shining from the water that did not sit well with my nerves. In all that rocking, we lost a seat and a paddle but finally got loose and made it to the shore. I swore to myself that I would never be in that pond again after dark. However, as soon as we made it back to the cabin, I immediately became relaxed again. I will always remember the special times that I have shared with Poppy at the country.

One January, Poppy and Bernie decided to have a son-in-law weekend. I had never met Bernie's son-in-law, Brad, but we hit it off well once he finally found the cabin. He got lost on the way to the country, which is not hard to do. We had a great time laughing, talking, and fishing. Poppy and Bernie introduced us to the nightly "cough medicine" tradition. That memorable weekend started making me think of how wonderful it is that the country experience has been passed down from generation to generation.

Lee, Justin's daughter, and I are blessed to have two boys, Will and Ross. These boys have heard about the country since birth and could not wait to be old enough to go on a "boys weekend." If they hear that anyone is heading that way, then they are ready to go! My two boys and I, along with my brother-in-law, Mark, and his son, Elliott, have started our own traditions. We go to the country Thanksgiving night every year to stay for the entire weekend and have made some great memories with our sons that can never be replaced. As a matter of fact, my entire extended family joined us there for Thanksgiving dinner this year. We laughed, walked through the woods, shot skeet, and just enjoyed each other and our surroundings.

In closing, to me, the country means special memories of family, old friends, new friends, and fun!

Brad Mclean
(Ordained Baptist Pastor)

I grew up in the small, middle Georgia town of Fort Valley and have hunted, fished, and enjoyed the outdoors all my life. So a visit to the country was probably not as foreign to me as it might be to a lot of visitors. I went with Bernie, my father-in-law, and Justin brought his son-in-law, Ryon. In addition to the comradeship that we enjoyed, Ryon and I had another thing in common. Our wives, Bernie's and Justin's daughters, are the same age and have been friends for many years.

We were there during hunting season, so in addition to fishing, we had a dove shoot. However, it wasn't very productive. Just four of us couldn't cover a two-hundred-acre field adequately, so the doves weren't at much risk. But we did have country skeet practice as we took turns shooting our shotguns at Coke cans that were tossed into the air. The fishing was also probably not as productive as usual because a winter cold front moved in on us. I remember waking up about 3:00 am the first night with my head freezing. I looked up, saw an open window, and thought, *What in the world is that window doing open?* I asked Bernie about it the next morning, and he said he liked it that way. The old guys caught a few more than we did due to their years of experience, and I guess they had learned to handle the cold better than I had.

You may have already read Bernie's account of our visit entitled "The Sons-in Law." Here is my response to that: he's a fine Christian man who never lies, but if you know him well, you quickly realize that he has a God-given talent to make more out of something than was really there. On second thought, that gift probably has been given to all serious fishermen!

Even though the fish weren't very active, the doves wouldn't fly our way, and the weather didn't cooperate, the fun, fellowship, and food could not have been better. I can really see why these old fellows called the Bass Buddies love going to the country.

Bass Buddies with (Top) John; (Middle), Bucky; (Bottom) Richard.

Reflections and Conclusions

WE MENTIONED IN THE beginning that we put this little book together with mixed emotions. Time has taken its toll on all of us, so chances are we won't be together in "the country" again. But what a wonderful privilege it is for us to relive some of our most memorable experiences through this little volume. As we read each other's tales, we are reminded of a special place, a special time, and special people. Our individual lives have been enriched, and a bond has been created among the four of us and the others who have joined us over the years. So we depart by reminding you of the five F-words that we hope to convey in this modest effort to record our adventures.

First, we've had a lot of *fun* as we shared these life experiences with each other. Our senses of humor have expanded and matured. We have learned to laugh at and with each other and, probably more importantly, to laugh at ourselves. During our trips almost every night before going to bed, someone would share a good story. This would set the stage for the next morning—waking up to another fun-filled day.

Second, *folly* doesn't usually have a good connotation. The word can imply foolishness, silliness, and the like on someone's part. But to us, there is a positive side to this little word. Sometimes it is just downright liberating and therapeutic for grown men to take off their masks and facades and just be themselves. There is nothing wrong with being a bit foolish and silly and even less refined and sophisticated from time to time. It allows old men like us to act young again.

Third, very few things on this earth are cherished more than *friendship*. Friends know you yet still love you; they will tell you what you need to hear, even if it's not what you want to hear. You can be yourself around friends, and they are there when needed. Women probably nurture these relationships better than men. However, when men are together during concentrated times like our trips, the relationships change from mere acquaintances to lasting friendships. What a fellowship we have enjoyed. And we've got each other's backs.

Fourth, individually and collectively, *faith* is so important. The four of us are at different points in our walk with the Lord. That would be the case with any group. But in a way, that is helpful to us all. We have shared important things with each other, we have prayed together, and in a unique way, we have even worshiped and acknowledged God's presence with us. There's something special about spending quality time together with Christian brothers.

And finally, *fishing* brought us together in a unique way. This great sport has interesting requirements for success. Certainly, the body of water must have an adequate population of game. The fisherman must have some skills and expertise. These include understanding the fish's habits, what bait to use, how to make a good cast or presentation, and of course, patience, persistence, etc. Interestingly, even when everything seems to be right, there have been times when one, two, or all of us failed to catch fish. We have a term for this: *skunked*. Each one of us has been skunked from time to time, and this reminds us of an old adage: "That's why they call it 'fishing' and not 'catching.'"

Catching fish is just icing on the cake. Men by nature can be tough, demanding, competitive, and even self-centered. But we have found that time away together sharing, encouraging, eating, drinking "cough medicine," and oh yes, fishing results in a special bond. You see, the cake is the pure joy and blessing of being part of a band of brothers. We have a parting tradition each time we leave the country; we give each other a bear hug and say, "I love you, brother!"

We hope you enjoyed the adventures of the Bass Buddies and our tales of fun, folly, friendship, faith, and even a little fishing.

Bass Buddies' Photo Album

(Top) John, Justin, and Bernie; (Bottom) Bernie and Robert.

(Top) Justin, Robert, and Bernie; (Middle) Earl; (Bottom) First trolling motor.

(Top) Bass Buddies in front of the Cowarts' cabin; (Bottom) Bernie, Richard, and John.

Bass Buddies' Mounted Trophies

(Top) Bernie's at home and (Bottom) at Lake Junaluska.

(Top) Robert's piranha and (Bottom) with his bass.

(Top) Earl's and (Bottom) Justin's.

Bass Buddies' Art Gallery

(Top) Rendering of the cabin by Annette Rigdon Swan;
(Bottom) original Prohibition sign at the country.

(Top) Painting by Annette Rigdon Swan of Frank and Justin Burgstiner with Bernie from 1955 photo;

(Bottom) Deason's Lake became known as the "pond."

Books By Bernie Brown

Lessons Learned on the Way Down: A Perspective on Christian Leadership in a Secular World

"These highly readable recollections will touch your heart and help you bridge the gap between your career path and faith journey." **Ken Blanchard**, Coauthor of The One Minute Manager

Purpose in the Fourth Quarter: Finishing the Game of Life Victoriously

"We all could be well served by adding this little volume to our 'playbooks.'" **Raymond Berry**, NFL wide receiver, head coach, Pro Football Hall of Famer

Snookie and Bernie Are Sweethearts: An Anatomy of a Marriage
Coauthored with wife, Snookie

"They make an incredible pair, yielding higher results in their life together than either could have produced alone." **Jenny Brown Bailey**, the Browns' firstborn

Road Signs on the Journey Home; Fifty-Two Modern-Day Proverbs

"Now grab your hat and coat. Watch the road! Bernie will take you on a ride that can change your life." **Dr. Sam Matthews**, Senior Minister, First United Methodist Church, Marietta, GA

Visit www.purposeinthefourthquarter.com

Or www.inspiringvoices.com (bookstore)

Or amazon.com/books or other book sellers

Bernie's email address: bernielb@bellsouth.net

Printed in the United States
By Bookmasters